# BECAUSE I CARE...

## Inspiration for Caregiving for Spouses, Health Care Personnel, Family & Friends

**The Spiritual Strengths Healing Plan**

Richard P. Johnson, Ph.D.

ISBN 978-0-9895130-8-1

10 9 8 7 6 5 4 3 2 1

First Edition

*Cover design by Megan Irwin*

*Edited by Maggie Singleton*

Printed in the United States of America

# BOOKS IN THE SPIRITUAL STRENGTHS HEALING SERIES

by Richard P. Johnson

- God Give Me Strength! Finding the Inner Power to Turn Your Illness/Brokenness/Life Transition Around
- Discover Your Spiritual Strengths: Find Health, Healing, and Happiness (flagship book of the Spiritual Strengths Healing Plan)
- Body, Mind, Spirit: Tapping the Healing Power Within
- Prayers for Spiritual Strength: Physical Illnesses, Emotional Broken Places, and/or Spiritual Dis-eases
- The Ten Most Effective Self-Care Healing Techniques: What You Can Do to Maximize Your Healing Journey
- The Power of Smiling: Using Positive Psychology for Optimal Health & Healing
- Healing Wisdom: 101 Spiritual Truths for Healing Your Illness
- Healing and Depression: Finding Peace in the Midst of Transition, Turmoil, or Illness
- Staying Spiritually Centered for Optimal Healing: Even When You're Sick or Life Seems Out of Control
- Seeking Significance: How to Discover New Self-Direction and New Life-Purpose Beyond Your (Unwanted) Life Transition

**Caregiving Titles**

- Caregiving from Your Spiritual Strengths: The Ten Fundamental Principles for Optimal Success
- Because I Care...Inspiration for Caregiving for Spouses, Health Care Personnel, Family & Friends

# The Spiritual Strengths Healing Plan

The Spiritual Strengths Healing Plan allows you to harness your internal healing power! It is not "faith healing" in which one relies on divine intervention as the sole means for physical cure, nor does it promise cure. Its purpose is healing and is best seen as a supplement to and support for current medical practices. The Spiritual Strengths Healing Plan's philosophy holds that each individual needs to seek the best and most appropriate medical and psychological care they can, in accord with their own personal wishes, and supplement their care with this Plan.

Please note that you will see the word "illness" throughout this book in its broadest sense and may indicate any (or a combination) of the following:

## *I. Physical Sicknesses*

Cancer, heart disease, MS, Lupus, migraine, addictions, hypochondriasis, pain, weight management/loss, smoking cessation, pneumonia, COPD, hypertension, arthritis, immune disorders, Parkinson's, diabetes, stroke, chronic fatigue etc., etc.

## *II. Psychological Issues*

Anxiety, depression, personality disorders, OCD, manipulation, stress, bi-polar disorder, etc., etc.

### *III. Emotional Issues*

Being unrealistic, lacking responsibility, low-self-esteem, career focus issues, poor organization skills, family disharmony, anger management, fears, perfectionism, marriage discontent, lifelessness, infidelity, irritability, chronic lateness, caregiving, etc., etc.

### *IV. Spiritual Dis-eases*

Peace of mind and heart, un-forgiveness, existential angst, inner pain, grudges, scrupulosity, incomplete developmental transitions, guilt, grief and unresolved grief, regrets, blame, disappointments, so-called "unfinished business," resentments, etc., etc.

### *V. Spiritual Direction & Growth*

Gaining better clarity of God's plan in your life, and breaking through barriers that may be hindering your faith journey.

*Where do <u>you</u> need healing?*

*For more information about the Spiritual Strengths Healing Plan, log on to...*

*<u>www.SpiritualStrengthsHealing.com</u>*

**The Spiritual Strengths Healing Institute**

*Learning the art of healing for self and others*

# Contents

# Introduction

You need this little book of inspirations because you've been called to care for another who is dealing with some type of illness (physical, psychological, emotional, or spiritual). Whether you are the spouse of a patient, a family member, a medical care professional, or an in-home volunteer or a paraprofessional caregiver, your call is a very large part of your life right now. Perhaps you've never thought of your caring work as a call, but make no mistake that it is. You want to do your very best. Caregiving includes those who give direct care, whether that be in your home, in private care, in-hospital care, in retirement centers or otherwise, but it also includes emotional care that may be given in-person or offered from a geographic distance.

Answering a call is much more than performing a job. A call implies something higher, something more meaningful, and even something spiritual, all folded together into the mix of motivation that brought you to this "place" to undertake this work. Regardless of how you see your call, as strictly human, or one with spiritual dimensions, the result is the same; you are here and tasks need to be accomplished. Yet, how you see your caregiving work makes a vast difference in your mental and emotional state, the manner in which you perform your caregiving tasks, and the degree of "heart" that you place in them.

The path to caregiving is varied; some caregivers choose their caregiving role with a clear intention of helping; others "back into" their caregiver role with no preparation and no intention on their part at all; still others "accept" it because there is no one else to do it. Regardless of your motivation, and regardless of the particular set of circumstances that brought you to this role, the fact is that you are here. By your choice or not... the role is yours.

What follows is my attempt to offer you an inspiring set of new attitudes of positivism. This book is intended to be your "on-call" reference, and your "go-to" manual for daily inspiration. You can use it in several ways: 1) as a casual read, 2) as a study, or 3) as one care idea a day—allowing it to saturate your caregiving attitudes throughout the day, and letting the ideas shape and direct you and your care accordingly.

## *Background*

I've been studying caregiving and personally caring for caregivers for some time now. My first book on caregiving, Parenting Your Aging Parents was published in 1987, when I was the Director of Behavioral Sciences at a large teaching medical center. I noticed that there was a continuous flow of patients who came through our ambulatory care center who were presenting with such things as head pain, back pain, gut pain, irritable bowel syndrome, fatigue, spastic colon, insomnia, anxiety, depression, and a litany of "vague" symptoms. These disorders, and many others, can be described as having a strong component of psycho-social involvement. That means that some factors in the equation of their sickness could be attributed to distress in some area of the patient's life. I decided to investigate this phenomenon further.

What I found in very short order was that over 90% of these patients had some form of caregiving responsibilities. Could it be that caregiving itself was putting a significant amount of distress on these patients to actually disturb their internal health-balancing mechanisms enough to push them over into sickness? This seemed plausible. Investigations that I subsequently undertook of this question proved that caregiving, when inappropriately practiced, can cause sickness. Furthermore, by almost every parameter of sickness, caregivers as a group exhibit more illness than non-caregivers. At one point I hosted 16 caregivers support groups to help caregivers be all they could be in the demanding role into which they had been thrust. I learned many, many things about caregiving from those wonderful people.

This is now my fifth book on caregiving. It is different from previous ones because I've learned how much caregiving comes from the heart more than from the head. In this volume I'm aiming at your heart; I'm trying to provide inspiration rather than simply listing, describing, and showing how to perform caregiving tasks better. I've found that the foundation of caregiving is spiritual, that the best caregiving is done as a "soul endeavor" that involves one's head, one's heart, and one's faith in something bigger than oneself. I can only hope that this small volume helps you be balanced of head, compassionate of heart, and illuminated of soul.

## *Care Receiver*

Because I intend this book for both 1) family caregivers who give care in the home context and 2) professional caregivers in the hospital, clinic, or extended medical care settings, I use the awkward term **"**care receiver**"** to designate the person (or persons) dealing with illness to whom you give care. The "care receiver" designation refers to both, 1) caregiving in the home setting, whether this care is given directly or only indirectly, AND 2) caregiving in the medical setting, regardless of their "stripe." A caregiver and a care receiver together form a team; each is a partner on this team. I apologize for the unfortunate awkwardness of the phrase, but I felt I had no choice. Thank you!

I also use the generic "**she**" and "**her**" to describe both genders. I felt I couldn't give you another potentially confusing designation such as **s/he**, or **he/she**, or **his/her**, or **her/his** to contend with. Again, I offer you my apology for this second awkwardness. I chose the female designation simply because I thought male designation of "he" and "him" seemed sexist on my part. Thank you X2!

I've written this volume in the first person singular. I did this to emphasize the intimacy of the caregiving role. Essentially the role is a set of interactions between a caregiver and the care receiver. The role is an immediate, personal, and quite individual engagement that demands not only your service but also requires you to use your own personality and your very self, in the mix.

## *Healing vs. Curing*

Please take note that I use the word healing throughout the book. This is quite intentional in that I draw a strict separation between *healing* on the one hand, and *curing* on the other. *Curing* refers to what the medical community hopes to offer; it hopes to cure the sickness. *Healing* is very different. Healing seeks to close the chasm that has opened up in your care receiver as a reaction to their sickness. The overall mission of the **Spiritual Strengths Healing Plan** is to help heal illness of whatever type—those personal, emotional, psychological, and/or spiritual reactions that can often flow from a sickness. A short list of illnesses might include anger, depression, anxiety, shame, guilt, irritability, hard heartedness, indifference, obtuseness, weakness, insecurity, etc., etc., etc. Pain comes from both sickness and illness. Therefore, when we help one, we also help the other.

This book speaks the language of healing, and it allows you to do the same. This language of healing is imbedded in the content of the 30 "care themes." These 30 are based on the 30 healing spiritual strengths identified in a study I conducted that uncovered why some hospital patients seem to heal better than others. The answer was so surprising as to be almost unbelievable—they healed better because they tapped into their unique spiritual strengths!

The study determined that your spiritual strengths provide the dynamic power required for healing. This dramatic healing discovery prompted a flurry of efforts to refine and catalogue the results of the study into a coherent and practical system of healing, which has been used by thousands of persons suffering from a variety of physical, emotional, and spiritual disorders. This book is the first time that these 30 spiritual strengths have been applied in the caregiving arena. These 30 spiritual themes of caregiving are presented here in the order they appear in the flagship "text" of the ***Spiritual Strengths Healing Plan***, Discover Your Spiritual Strengths.

You will notice that under each of the 30 care themes you'll find three words. The middle word is the spiritual strength. The word to the right is the shadow of that spiritual strength.

A shadow is a condition of absence of the strength. The word to the left is the compulsion of that strength.

A compulsion is a perversion of the spiritual strength—how your ego might distort the spiritual strengths and use it for its own purposes. This is all described in Discover Your Spiritual Strengths.

Spiritual strengths are ideals; they represent the pinnacle of excellence in caregiving. But please remember: NO ONE ACHIEVES EXCELLENCE ALL THE TIME. Excellence is a state of perfection that we can only strive for and never fully achieve in any consistent way. The very worst consequence of this book would be if, as you read, you judge yourself as lacking because you don't measure up to this virtue ideal.

We walk into the caregiving arena quite human, which means we bring along with us not only our strengths but also our vulnerabilities, our fears, and reactions to our fears (shadows and compulsions). We certainly strive for excellence, knowing fully that it is an elusive goal, but it is still our best model and one worth the effort. Our journey toward excellence vastly enhances our caregiving experience—not just for our care receiver but just as importantly it enhances us. Striving for excellence allows us to remain positive, motivated, invigorated, and most of all, it allows us to see our care as a call.

Using this volume as your caregiving handbook and truly embracing the essence of what is being said, will contribute mightily to your becoming an agent of hope and healing for your care receiver. Using the ideas herein as the framework of your caregiving can transform your care work from a potentially morbid sequence of increasingly depressing care tasks to a profound spiritual adventure of personal growth. The 30 care themes are like hidden gems woven into the fabric of care that you progressively unfold to discover the awesome wonders of Love.

You are as unique as a fingerprint, so not every sentence, every thought, every emotion or situation mentioned in this book will directly apply to your caregiving situation, certainly not. You will not feel the same feelings or encounter the issues that other caregivers do. As you proceed through this book, try not to judge yourself by every sentence, rather pick the ones that do apply to you and try to discern exactly how you might be uniquely expressing this concept.

## *Your Spiritual Strengths*

I make reference to "Spiritual Strengths" throughout the book. What are Spiritual Strengths? Each of us is gifted with special strengths quite unique to our one-of-a-kind personality. The overall purpose or goal of your personality is to express the uniqueness of you. To accomplish this lifelong task, your personality is powered by grace (spiritual strengths). With this grace-power, your personality is constantly performing six functions, of which you are almost entirely unaware. These six are 1) believing, 2) perceiving, 3) thinking, 4) feeling, 5) deciding, and 6) acting. Each one of these six personality functions is energized by a different spiritual strength. Your six spiritual strengths together provide the energy necessary to heal your illness.

## *Spiritual Strengths Healing Profile (SSHP)*

You can discover your unique six spiritual strengths by consulting www.spiritualstrengthshealing.com. There you will find how to take the **Spiritual Strengths Healing Profile** (**SSHP**), a 120-item, valid and reliable questionnaire that will, in your personal 20-page report, scientifically pinpoint and describe not only your six "premier" spiritual strengths, but also bring you on a journey of self-knowledge unlike any other, which will propel you forward toward optimal living and caregiving excellence.

I wish you every blessing in your call to caregiving. Illness is dauntless in its ongoing effects on the body, mind, and spirit. Caregiving is punctuated with almost every emotion possible—from anger to empathy, from frustration to patience, from profound sadness to irrepressible joy, and many, many more. If you are like other caregivers, you will come to learn that this is true. We must learn to care for ourselves... this is the central goal of this book: to teach you how to honor another without dishonoring yourself.

---

***A Final Note:***

*I am a Christian by birth and practice, and I have no doubt that this lifetime faith walk shows through in these pages. Please don't infer from this bias that this book is only for Christians. I believe that the truths in these pages are universal. I've written them from a Christian perspective because it's the only one that is natural for me. If you are not a Christian, then I ask you to filter my bias so that my words ring clear and true to you. I thank you.*

---

*Richard P. Johnson, Ph.D.*

# 30

## Because I Care… Statements

ONE

---

# *Because I Care…*
# *I know the Spirit is with me in every caregiving encounter.*

---

At the core of my being is the rock-solid center point of the Spirit. My indwelling Spirit provides me with all the power and all the strength that I now require in my call to caregiving.

I rely on this Spirit for all my energy to see and think, to feel and decide, and finally to act. All of this motivation and inspiration is from the Spirit. My call to caregiving was a special call to find new growth and spiritual development. I strive to be ever centered in and on the Spirit.

I depend on the Spirit's guidance and care of me. I remain open to the Spirit's continuing call, the true lead of my uniqueness. I am secure knowing that my Inner Spirit is my secure undergirding.

All my innermost surety, confidence, and security flow from my Inner Spirit's strength in me.

While caring for my care receiver is more than tough at times, it does allow me to discover hidden strengths within me—the power and might of the Spirit ever-present within me.

Strength does not originate in me, but the Spirit's strength is in me. I can use this power in each and every caregiving encounter. I know I'm not alone as I care for my care receiver; the Spirit within cares for me.

The Spirit gives me energy to fortify me for the sometimes daunting task of caregiving, and so I can pass on the power my spiritual strengths to my care receiver. I am left better, enhanced in mood and calm in spirit, when I allow the Spirit's energy (grace) to flow over me and through me.

When I am fully "with" the Spirit in me, there is no room for doubt. Certainly I question myself and I question what is; but my questioning leads me to the mystery of life—that I am part of the circle of life, the inhalation and exhalation of the Spirit in me.

I know I'm fallible, I do make mistakes, I sometimes feel uncertain and distrustful, but I always eventually find rest and comfort within when things get tough. Sometimes, in my doubt, I try to control the uncontrollable and I'm left lonely and cold before I once again return to union with my spiritual center point.

# TWO

***Because I Care…***

***I put my needs aside and focus on my care receiver's needs first.***

How often do I ask myself, "*What am I doing*?" The question carries both honesty, a true desire to do my best in caregiving, and no small level of vanity as in *"Perhaps I'm better than to do this!"*

Caregiving requires that I gently set my ego aside and concentrate on my care receiver's needs. I know I'm performing the role of caregiver, but it's much more than simply performing tasks. It requires the best of my entire personality—my best perceptions, thoughts, and feelings.

I'm called to be humble, but this is not a humility undermined by any submissiveness or resignation; rather it's a full-bodied humility free of playing roles and wearing masks to cover up any of my foibles. Caring is my classroom for learning who I am; it teaches me the real me; it can also activate my "not attractive side" of self-centeredness.

It's true, I can be vain and prideful, and I can put myself first at times. Yet caring calls me to use my personality in service of another. I just can't take this to the extreme of losing myself in the caregiving process.

There is nothing about caregiving that forces me to put myself down, to feel inferior or shameful. I need to remember that balanced caregiving builds me up; it strengthens me by calling forth my best parts: the caring me. Caregiving shows me a new avenue of learning the "truth" about me.

Caring for my care receiver uncovers what's most real in me, but while I may become scared, upset, irritable, and even forlorn at times, I know that I'm not alone—the Spirit is always with me.

Certainly I falter when I neglect myself, or chastise myself, or see other "lacks" in me I'd rather not recognize. But, there they are, and what will be my reaction? Will I judge myself weak and insignificant, or will I recognize the true reality of me—the place of true humility at the Spirit-center of me?

Caregiving is my psychological and spiritual sandpaper. It smoothes my rough edges, it shapes me into being more "me" than I have been, and it doesn't pervert me into something I'm not. Caring teaches me that I can defer my needs; I can lay them aside as I minister to my care receiver's needs.

Here is the holy process of healing, both for my care receiver and for me. As I gradually learn that what I thought were "lacks" in me, which I needed to hide are but proofs of the center value of my Spirit-given strengths.

THREE

# *Because I Care… I honor my care receiver as a unique rendition of God's grace.*

*"To know you is to love you."* I can't honor my care receiver unless I know her; and to genuinely know I must first accept.

Acceptance has no hint of resignation, no disappointment, no sense that my care receiver or her behavior should be different. No, acceptance means I'm called to give my care receiver (and myself) my complete "*amen*" my complete *"so be it."*

I can't carry around a toxic sense of enmity or even disapproval. My care receiver is who she is, and her behavior is what it is. When I can accept this obvious reality I am complying with the truth of the situation.

When my care receiver acts like a curmudgeon then I accept her curmudgeon-ness and act accordingly. What I don't do is somehow resent it, try to correct it, consciously fight against it, or hold it against her. I acknowledge the reality of the situation and if necessary, rise above it; I do not let it work against my soul.

I learn to see that this behavior is part of the abundance of the Spirit's care for me; it may not be the most attractive part of the universal abundance (in my opinion), but nonetheless it is something that can be my spiritual teacher, and in that sense it is sacred.

I do not judge; I do not dissent. Caring for my care receiver requires a certain surrender of my ego self, my call to care requires that I put myself aside so I can more fully appreciate the singular uniqueness of my care receiver.

When I internally dissent I cause conflict within me, I provoke internal anger, I fragment myself, and eventually I find myself in open, yet internal warfare with my care receiver; this pushes me to want to break with her, in which case we both lose.

Likewise I cannot react to behavior I don't like by being aloof. I can't distance myself from giving care, I can't withdraw, or detach from the person of my care receiver. I can step away from any noxious behaviors my care receiver gives me, but I must not step away from the innate sacredness of the person of my care receiver.

My care receiver is much, much more than her behaviors. I can't only be "nice" to persons who are "nice" to me. I'm called to accept all there is in my care receiver, the good, the bad, and even the ugly.

I can't give a cold shoulder to my care receiver, or any other passive-aggressive behavior. I know who I am, a child of the Spirit, and as such I'm given to a higher calling. Yet, I'm never called to be dishonored, abused, or shamed by my care receiver. Walking this line between acceptance and abuse is a matter for continuous prayer.

FOUR

# *Because I Care…*
# *I look for ways of being more fully present to my care receiver.*

Caregiving means practicing established ways of being "present" with and for another, and finding new ways as well. Caregiving requires that I open myself to the sacred "now" of my care receiver. I'm attentive to her needs on all levels; I give credence to wants and desires as well as needs.

Caregiving requires that I exercise mercy. When I'm merciful I'm giving of myself—expressing my own giftedness and finding fulfillment therein. Merciful caring means I forgive lapses, or slights, or even frustration and anger in my care receiver: I also forgive myself for the same.

I'm relenting. I can let go of expectations and the judgments and criticism from my care receiver and myself. I'm mercifully caring when I can look my care receiver in the eyes, when I "touch" her with my words and actions, and when I understand her feelings.

My efforts at being fully present are blocked any time I withhold my attention. This sends a signal to my care receiver that I'm disregarding and even disrespecting—I'm simply going through the motions of care without being caring, without being fully present. As a *care*giver, I can't allow myself to be content with mediocrity.

I communicate inattentiveness when I don't follow through and don't accent my caregiving tasks with a smile, a touch, a word of tenderness, or at least a nod of interest in their "world." I isolate my care receiver by giving no eye contact, and/or being cold or blunt with my words. Any indifference on my part communicates an uncaring (and sometimes rude) demeanor that sets-up an atmosphere of alienation.

I can also violate basic principles of quality care when I carry out my care in an officious, detached, routinized, and perfunctory manner. Such behavior screams indifference to my care receiver. Anytime I'm hard-hearted, stubborn, punitive, or harsh, I damage the caring relationship that I'm authentically committed to establish and maintain.

I do all this in service of my care receiver certainly, but also because I want to be merciful and "present" to my own needs as well. A tenderly constructed care environment serves me also, as well as the Spirit in me, and in my care receiver.

FIVE

# *Because I Care... I have absolute assurance in the Spirit's healing power.*

Every time I approach my care receiver I bring either virtue or vice, either happiness or lifelessness, either hope or indifference. Because I do care... I choose to bring hope.

I want to live in hope myself, and so if I can consciously carry hope with me when I interact with my care receiver, and intentionally offer this hope, then I enhance my spirit and elevate my mood. When I bring hope, I demonstrate my honest assurance that the Spirit is "in charge" of healing. I bring my conviction that all will be well even in the face of duress and turmoil.

Hope communicates that healing will happen. This is not a false hope that a miracle cure is sure to occur soon, but an honest hope that Divine Will does eventually prevail, and that healing will bring peace of mind, heart, and soul. My hope suggests that there is fairness and goodness, and even cheer in the most distressing situations.

The spiritual call of illness is a silent call, yet it sometimes screams for attention in my heart. I believe this is equally true for my care receiver and for me as the caregiving. Hope is as perennial as the spring grass, and I'm very conscious of caring for my own sacred lawn by keeping in touch with my Inner Spirit.

I am optimistic; I expect the best to happen for my care receiver even when things look grim, and I communicate this infectious message in my words, my tone of voice, and in my total way of being with my care receiver.

It's hard sometimes to remain emotionally "up." I can become dispirited, heavy, somber, and yes, even gloomy at times. But I'm learning that even in these emotional shadow lands I can find hope, spirit, and light when I remember to put the Spirit into my life's equation. I can turn to the Spirit and rest my troubles there.

I can't simply presume that the Spirit will fix things according to my plan; I can never take the Spirit for granted. I can't be blind or assume unrealistic liberties with my caregiving time, energies, or resources; but I can call on that compelling force of life within me that always pulses positive prayers of hope that offer me safety, solace, and sacredness.

This assurance is real; it is divine healing power that resides in me by the mysterious working of the Spirit. While I have no entitlement to hope, I do have hope as part of my inheritance, and the assurance that hope does indeed spring eternal. I have hope in hope.

SIX

---

# *Because I Care… I seek to discover my care receiver's true personhood.*

---

My call to caregiving is not a call to perform tasks for the sake of the work, but rather it is an invitation to participate in the fullness of life. I wish to see the broad breadth of the human experience. I wish to see from a higher vantage point and take in the grandeur and the simplicity of what is good, true, and even beautiful.

When I see the world through spiritual eyes, the eyes that see deeper meaning, then all of this grandeur opens up to me. I see my care receiver not as dependent with a never-ending list of needs, not as an endless to-do list of tasks, but rather as a graced person who, while she does have many needs, is also the depository of an interesting life, a personal history of stories, an emotional and psychological amalgam of curiosity, and a valued member of a family.

Yet even more, my care receiver is a unique assemblage of the Spirit's craft—intentionally created and carefully guarded over the years. I'm called by my care role to come to as clear an awareness of my care receiver as I can, not so much for her, but more so that I can experience the full-bodied richness of her, and in so doing live a more complete life myself.

I need to see my care receiver's journey with illness as her opportunity to reach out and find the Spirit's hand that has been outstretched all along. My care receiver is a big part of my current lived experience, and I'm called to find that hand of the Spirit too. I'm called to see a glimpse of heaven in this person.

I must see beyond what my physical senses offer me, beyond the material plane; I want to capture the "very much more" that resides in my care receiver. I want to expand my limited perception and see the depth of spirit, the breadth of soul, and the expanse of grace that continuously courses through my care receiver—even if my care receiver is no longer cognitively in-touch with everyday reality, even when my care receiver is mentally diminished.

I don't want my vision blocked; no, I wish to see the whole picture of my care receiver; I want no failure of focus, nor any lazy sightedness to dim the light that resides in my call to care.

I wish to see the fuller meaning, the true meaning of my caring work. I don't want my eyes to deceive me by focusing on the tasks of care alone, much more so I want to see the treasures of care.

SEVEN

---

# *Because I Care... I try to remain light and bright with my care receiver.*

---

People are funny, and so is my care receiver. Yes, people are funny in the sense of being "strange" at times, confusing at other times. But people are also funny, or can be funny, in a humorous way as well. Can I see the humor in the broader human condition?

Sometimes I simply shake my head in an incredulous smile reacting to some piece of behavior that can only make sense when I inject humor into it. My caring role is packed with humor; it's all there for me to see, or not, all there in a sometimes absurdly funny unfolding of levity right before my eyes.

At such times I can choose to be exasperated or amused; I can become irritated or find it comical; I can roll my eyes in disgust or roll them in delight—it's truly up to me! I do want my call to care to be fun, even when the tasks I'm called to perform seem anything but funny.

I want to see the light side, I want to find the levity that's always there if I let it peek through, I want to see delight, and I want to laugh—not at my care receiver's ineptness, but laugh *with* her. I want to appreciate the many moments of amusement and not lose them.

I don't want to see myself as a trapped victim of circumstances beyond my control, I don't want to lament either my work or the fact that I've been called to it. I don't' want to pity my care receiver; instead I want to laugh with her. I want to smile not frown, I want to be "up" and not down.

Illness can bring my care receiver to her knees, and the pain of it all can open rivers of tears. My smile is a reminder of a brighter time, and a reassurance that she is not alone. I never want to lose hope that something wonderful is about to begin, and that something wonderful has so much to do with how clearly I can see humor in myself—in my foibles and mistakes, my weaknesses and my stumbles, and in my attempts just to be me.

On the other hand, I don't wish to hide behind my humor, to make a joke out of everything or, to be so light that my feet aren't grounded in reality. It's been said that humor is sometimes the face of wisdom. When I see the grand humor in the human condition—when I train myself to see the amusing cheer that's always there—then I've stepped into a new arena of understanding that brightens my mood, nourishes my soul, and enlivens my spirit.

EIGHT

# *Because I Care... I work "with" my care receiver; not against her.*

What does it mean when we say to "work with" another? Certainly I expect to "work with" my care receiver so I can make something happen, accomplish a task, or perform a function. So much of my caregiving is "doing," performance, achievement, and accomplishing work.

To "work with" means that I expect my care receiver's cooperation, her assistance by being accommodating, and her, more or less, full attention to help me get the job done right. Another aspect of "working with" my care receiver is building a relationship with her: mutuality, respect, good communication, trust, and commitment combine in successful teamwork.

So much of what I do falls into the category of relationship building. I need a solid relationship to work with my care receiver. I need to know her, and to find an easy smoothness between us; at the very least this relationship needs to be a "working relationship" where we synchronize our mutual efforts to create something healthy, good, and even sacred.

Simply creating relationship is "doing enough" at times, and in order to create a helping relationship... to build the togetherness, the respect, the communication, the deeper understanding, the trust, and the shared commitment that are the hallmarks of a good relationship, I first need to establish a condition of peace and understanding.

Peace means we can be together in concord, where we feel a sense of mutual security and even serenity, where we can be quiet together, and where tranquility is the order of the day.

I see that in some paradoxical way, illness strips my care receiver's self away, while at the same time it is additive to her. I need to be with this simultaneous stripping and building process as my care receiver experiences it. When and where peace exists, then healthy relationship grows.

Sometimes I find peace difficult. Sometimes when I feel opposition or ridicule or just plan unhappiness in my care receiver, I can react defensively; I can be unfriendly, contrary, and even angry. When I sense such negative emotional reactions in me, then I know it's time to shift my approach.

I've strayed from peacemaking, and I've moved away from relationship building. It's my cue to shift, to step back and reassess. I'm usually reacting to something I've seen or sensed in my care receiver that invades my value system.

Sometimes I sense her opposition or confrontation or provocation. I don't want to work against my care receiver; I don't want to work against creating a healthy relationship (and ultimately against myself). I need to clarify my motivations and realign my efforts. I need to stop, contemplate the situation, and return to peace.

# NINE

## *Because I Care… I try to be a flexible palm tree; not a rigid oak tree.*

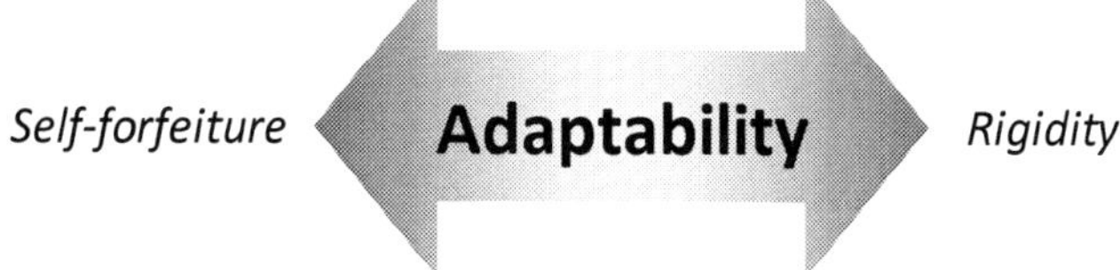

Caregiving calls me to sway, to flex, to bend, to adjust, to work around, to go with the flow, to be "light on my feet," and to always "test the emotional water" before jumping in. Yes, caregiving demands my personal flexibility, malleability, and most of all, it requires immense amounts of adaptability.

Adaptability is the very air of caregiving... it's that necessary for survival. I've learned to shift directions quickly, to choose the battles to lose so I can win the war, to conform to the moment, to adopt a broader perspective, and sometimes to move sideways in order to keep moving forward! Adaptability is indispensable.

I've learned that any rigidity from me disturbs my care receiver and disrupts the energy (grace) flow of the day. My care receiver wants me loose not tight, open not closed, accepting not critical, fluid not stiff, and flowing not stagnant.

Illness stuns my care receiver and it can overwhelm her and leave her powerless, but it also gives my care receiver the totally new opportunity to become open to the symphony of love emerging from within her. I play a role in this symphony by showing respect and kindness to her and to myself.

I need to be open and free so I can flow freely with her as these new symphonic movements begin to unfold. I know I can't close my ears and be harsh with my care receiver. Though sometimes I need to impose structure, I try to never impose stricture.

But I've found that perhaps my biggest internal battle is not creeping rigidity, as much as an advancing self-forfeiture. I fear I can sometimes lose myself in my efforts to remain adaptable. I can become so adaptable that I can give-in on necessary issues and give-up the natural power that a good caregiver requires.

I find myself overly-solicitous of my care receiver's needs; at times I find it difficult, if not impossible, to say "no;" I lose my self-direction; I negate what I know is right for me and for my care receiver; I can sometimes buckle under the constant pressure of hearing her wants repeated over and over; I doubt my own thinking, and I can even give up my sense of self.

Such a perversion of adaptability causes me much more worry and personal anguish than being rigid ever did. I can compromise too much, and I find it hard to re-discover the line that invisibly divides healthy adaptability from damaging self-forfeiture.

I struggle to find the balance in me that both honors adaptability yet maintains personal integrity; that allows positive relationship development, and that encourages caregiving productivity at the same time.

TEN

# *Because I Care... I keep my focus and my energies on the "main thing" of my care receiver.*

When I am with her, my care receiver's needs are my "main thing." Nothing is more important in that sacred "now" of our union than what we share together.

What is my care receiver's "main thing?" I'm called to be like a laser beam on her, giving her my full and undivided attention, the fullness of my focus. And I try to focus on her "main thing" of that particular moment.

The illness journey is full of tangled thorns and twisted brambles, but through it all I must keep my focus on what is most important, what is embedded in the process—my care receiver's growth into new life.

I come before my care receiver in simple honesty, in grace, and without pretense. It's as though I've been captivated by a child-like innocence seeking only goodness and cheer. I leave behind any preconceived notions that may divert my focus from the good of that moment; I break from the past and see only the "now," two people together in simple sharing, some interactions supported by words and some not.

My own world can be cluttered and overloaded; it can be pressured and confused; it can be disorganized and entangled, but for the moments I'm with my care receiver all of this complexity is left behind as I focus exclusively on her.

The intensity of my focus actually gives me relief from the ruffles of my life outside this encapsulated holy moment. I feel a new freedom emerging in my personality as the cares of the day slide off my shoulders and I'm left standing taller, seeing clearer, thinking cleaner, feeling nearer, and acting dearer.

This is what I cherish about my caregiving—time slows and I become more myself in this environment of simple beauty. I throw away any perceptions that might subvert this protected arena of simplicity. I refrain from quick assessments that may distort my vision; my motives are smooth and graceful.

I can focus on the details of my caring, but am keen to keep my tasks of care in the supportive position always additive to the bigger picture, the overall "main thing" of focusing on the person of my care receiver.

Tasks, while important, generally take a secondary position to relationship. My gaze is soft not blunt, my eyes are clear not blurred, and my demeanor is reverent ... almost sacred, as I remember that my "main thing" is seeing my caring role as my current call to personal purpose, emotional meaning, and spiritual authenticity.

ELEVEN

# *Because I Care…*
# *I remain faithful to my role and my experience.*

I know that I've been called to care. Time and circumstances, inner strengths, and outer talents have come together in this opportunity where I can express my uniqueness in the personal ministry of caregiving.

Certainly I could use my gifts and talents in other occupations or professions, but I'm confident that my call to caring is real; I have faith that I am where I should be.

I also have faith in the role of caregiving. I know, at least for now, that the role is necessary and important; it is authentic for me, and real for my care receiver.

At times, I doubt my loyalty; but then my Inner Spirit's voice restores my conviction that this is right, that I have much to learn here and immense inner growth to stretch for. I strive to be obedient to the role and to my current level of experience and expertise.

I'm keenly aware of my limits. I keep boundaries clear in my understanding of what I can do and what I can't, or at least shouldn't attempt. I know when to ask for assistance; I try hard not to over-extend myself.

I adhere to the established ways of care; I have faith in the Spirit's presence within me, and rely on that divine power for direction and support. I know that the Spirit's guiding hand is upon mine, and I take great solace in this active work in my caregiving role.

I try hard to maintain my caregiving course. I see the wisdom in established guidelines and abide by the rules—even though I can sometimes chaff under them. I'm faithful to the role and attempt to carry it out with an inner conviction and an outer dignity. I strive to be true to my call to care.

As a caregiver I stand vigil over the personal transformation that illness offers my care receiver. This transformation necessarily involves loss of what my care receiver thought of as her essential form. I am called to bear witness to this process.

I can sometimes become over-zealous; I can overdo my work when I get compulsively absorbed in it. I find the care mission a compelling one and may at times become somewhat overly focused on it, to a point where I might become carried away a bit with my desires to do my best and to press for ideas on how best to inject constructive change into the caregiving arena. I might even go so far in my compulsiveness that I actually try to change my care receiver's core personality.

Here again, I rely on my faith in the Spirit to bring me to my center point of peace and inner balance. Time and again I've seen this cycle of my own enthusiasm a bit over-extended, and then reigned-in to a place of inner stability where I find an ever-refreshing reminder of who I am and why I'm here, which renews me.

TWELVE

# *Because I Care… I strive to be and to do right.*

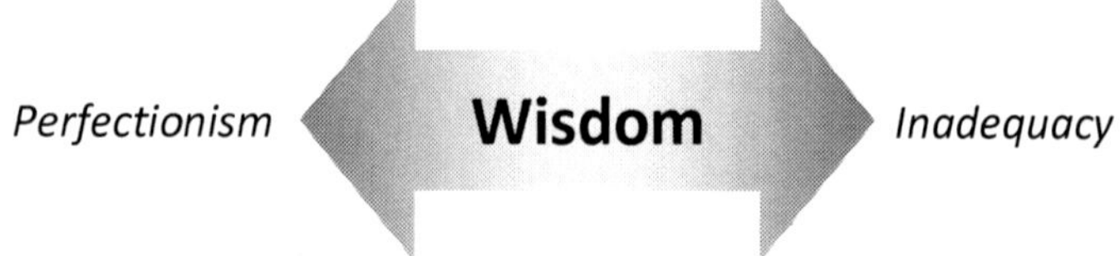

Naturally I want to do what's right. I do strive to follow a sensible, effective, and efficient course in my care work.

I'm clearly motivated to bring my background, study, observations, and experience together in as effective a manner and execution of caregiving excellence as I can. I try to use what I've learned in a wise manner for the greatest effect—not impulsively, wildly, or flippantly. I try to exercise solid insight as well as general good sense and considered judgment.

Illness brings my care receiver to a new poverty of spirit, a place where she feels naked and vulnerable; illness drives her out of the center point. Recognizing this reality motivates me to be and do right.

I want to function from my most enlightened core values to advance the overall vision and mission of care. All this, of course, is a tall order and I'm sometimes tempted to think that it's undoable (or at least unrealistic in today's world).

Sometimes I lack trust in myself and think that I'm not up to the job, that I'm "not enough." Such nagging thoughts unnerve me and cause an erosion of my confidence, which makes me feel shaky and unsure of myself.

Occasionally these thoughts of personal inadequacy or inferiority push me away from my center point of confidence and into a place where I seem to momentarily fall away from my usual calm and peaceful inner self-talk and toward a certain anxiety of soul.

This anxiety can extend beyond my own sense of self and gravitate to my caregiving role, where it creates doubt and uncertainty in me. I work hard to remove such inaccurate thoughts from my mind, but these thoughts can be stubborn; they want to hang around much longer than I'd like.

I know these thoughts are not true, they are not real; nonetheless they linger and can have some negative effect on my caregiving.

Sometimes I can even get into a mental “space” where I seem simply dissatisfied with my care work and with myself in the caregiving role.

My need to do "right" goes a bit overboard to the point where I become excessive in my demands of myself. I find I do more and more, but I’m still left feeling unfulfilled, with little sense of accomplishment.

This spiral can continue to a point where I expect "perfect" work and "perfect" caregiving from myself. I go quite beyond the standards of wisdom and enter into a place of haggard discontent.

Once again I need to return to my center, that tranquil place where the real me, the wise me, resides.

## THIRTEEN

# *Because I Care... I strive to be reliable and project a "you can count on me" image.*

Every day of my caregiving journey I learn and re-learn how to stand fast... how to be reliable. I want my care receiver to be secure knowing that I will be there for her; that I'll do what's in my power to show an internal steadfastness.

Reliability has different facets—one is communicating that physical care needs will be satisfied; another, perhaps as important an element of reliability, is showing that my care receiver can emotionally rely on me.

I notice my care receiver's feelings, emotions, and frames of mind; I make positive comment on her day, her views, and her interests. I'm time limited for sure, but I can be relied upon at least to recognize her psycho-emotional needs as well as her physical ones.

Caregiving calls me to be the best I can, to illuminate all the best that's in me so I can be reliable. Doing this, day after caring day, can generate a caregiving weariness that can numb my soul and cover my heart. I also need to care for me.

Within appropriate boundaries, I want my care receiver to know that her faith is safe with me. I will lift up her faith perspectives, but I will not evangelize; I will make a safe environment so she can feel free to state her faith beliefs—weaving them into the fabric of our interactions.

While I want to be resolute, steady, dependable, and purposeful all the time, it's not always possible. I can stumble over my own schedule, my own mindlessness, and my own laziness. I know that I suffer from omissions of dependability, oversights, and stress-related blocks that may prevent me at times from being the safe, reliable caregiver I wish to be.

I can get bogged-down in my own thoughts. I can become defensive, and even become a bit self-serving at times. All of this communicates certain failures of reliability that I fear my care receiver remembers perhaps even more than the many, many other times I am clearly dependable. This injects a certain uncertainty into the caregiving mix that I chronically battle. But a bigger threat to my steadfastness is my tendency to become fixated in my caregiving approach.

I can exaggerate or distort steadfastness by becoming fixated. I can show this in many ways: fearing change, dreading the unknown, turning a blind eye to a need for change, or by refusing to develop new approaches or gain more enlightened caregiving ideas, concepts, and skills. I can be stubborn at times and proverbially stick my head in the sand.

There is something in me that wants sameness, this both enhances reliability, while it also works against it. I know my care receiver wants and needs to depend on me, so I need to be reliable, but my attempts are somewhat erratic. I am a caregiving work in progress.

FOURTEEN

---

# *Because I Care…*
# *I strive to see the whole picture of my care receiver.*

---

I want to see my care receiver not simply as a bundle of care needs, not as a disease or diagnosis, not even as a patient. I want to see her as a full person with a complete personality just like anyone else.

I am tempted to see her only as a fragment of fullness, as neediness itself, as a broken, less-than-complete person. I know such thinking lacks integrity on my part in the sense that I fail to think of my care receiver as a completely integrated person, as having fullness in spite of her overload of needs that require my regular attention.

While she is physically diminished, I want to see my care receiver as personally and spiritually undiminished. This is particularly hard when any cognitive defects impair her ability to communicate fully.

Caregiving demands that I see the whole—the three systems of body, mind, and spirit as constantly interacting. The state of these three in unity or disunity powerfully influences the course of her illness. I try to help my care receiver achieve balance and cohesion among all three.

I need to keep in mind that I have no idea what's happening internally within her even during those times when it's hard to see much interaction externally. I need to remind myself that this person is undivided, full, and powerful at her core. As I gradually gain a bigger more global picture of my care receiver, I feel more integrated myself, I am enriched, I am made better, and I achieve a higher level of personality integration myself.

When I act with wholeness, I am rewarded by feeling whole myself; when I act fragmented I feel likewise—broken, divided, scattered, and irrelevant. If this emotional condition persists in me, I find that I can descend further; I can become discouraged, dispirited, unmotivated, and even broken as a caregiver.

I'm vulnerable at such times to turning my back on my caregiving role; I have thoughts that I'm fraudulent, I'm not what I appear or profess to be … I'm broken! I need to expand my narrow thinking, repair my broken thoughts about my care receiver and about my call to care. If I don't, I'm at risk of becoming dull and disinterested, aloof and indifferent, even petty and resistive.

I lose my real self all because I lose sight of the absolute, irrevocable fact that my care receiver is a full, complete, undivided person of worth and immense value (albeit one who has more needs at this time in her life).

I need to shake myself out of such limited, anemic, and illusionary thinking. I need to think coherently, with cohesion and purpose, integrity and unity. At times like these I depend entirely on the power and might of the Spirit within me who nudges me to wholeness again and again.

FIFTEEN

# *Because I Care… I always honor my care receiver.*

I am called to honor my care receiver. Certainly, honor speaks of being respectful, which includes unconditional benevolence on my part. I want to think the best about my care receiver.

Respect includes giving and expecting nothing in return, giving in a selfless manner, and anticipating the needs of my care receiver. Yet, there is another dimension of honoring that is captured in the precepts of many faith traditions, and that is the commandment to never abandon another person.

Clearly, physically abandoning my care receiver would be an extreme form of dishonor. Yet there are many other ways I can dishonor my care receiver beyond physical abandonment.

I can abandon my care receiver emotionally by not recognizing her feelings, not reinforcing her hopes, and not supporting her dreams. I can also abandon her psychologically by overlooking her unique personality, her personal and familial history, and any mental status issues, most notably: depression, anxiety, or any psychiatric care needs.

I can abandon my care receiver familially and socially by cutting off or neglecting her need to communicate with family and friends.

I can abandon my care receiver spiritually by not encouraging prayer and by overlooking her need to talk about spiritual matters—if not with me, then with someone qualified.

I can certainly dishonor my care receiver by being rude, ill natured, or critical. I can dishonor by my sharp tongue and acrid tone of voice, by my negative attitude, and by passivity of care. All these things, while stark when written down, are nonetheless quite common in many caregiving situations, and even creep into mine at times.

While honoring the illness condition certainly calls me to accept my care receiver's current emotional, psychological, and spiritual states; honoring also includes helping my care receiver to consider a profoundly deeper self-understanding... the entire illness experience can offer new life.

Yet there is another form of dishonor, and that form is directed at myself—I can't honor my care receiver by dishonoring myself. I dishonor myself, and my call to care, if and when I place myself in a submissive posture toward my care receiver. Whenever I feel slavish or subservient, or self-deprecating, or over-give to my care receiver, I am dishonoring myself, and my caring position.

Sometimes I want to help so much that I lose myself in the mix. Here is where I cross a line between giving genuine care, offending my caregiving role, and myself, and infantilizing my care receiver. Yet, through it all I remain charitable, giving of myself without expecting anything in return. Here is gift enough for me.

SIXTEEN

# *Because I Care…*
# *I feel and share the joy of being alive.*

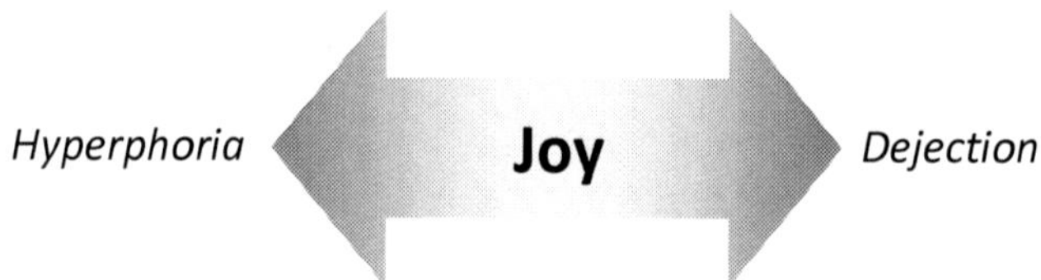

Caregiving makes me happy. There are times and places on my caregiving journey when and where I stop and pause for a bit and just look at my care receiver. Perhaps she is sleeping, or eating, or reading, or just watching TV, and I suddenly am struck by feeling a warm glow of inner pleasure wash over me.

I think of such times and such inner sensations as the Spirit's way of telling me that, "*All is well*," that "*This is right,*" that the Spirit is pleased with my care work. Such unspoken, very intimate times of joy feed my soul and re-charge me to carry on; they ground me in the Spirit's grace and reassure me that things are unfolding as they should.

I do feel joy answering the call to care, and I know that the Spirit's grace, power, and might sustain me through the day. I feel inwardly elated knowing that I will be sustained every day for my whole life.

My care receiver also needs to feel joy, yet joy's emergence requires comfort, safety, and protection—three caregiving goals I need to consider essential. My spirit is free and jubilant—my soul jumps for joy and I am glad and at peace.

But, dark clouds of sadness also gather around me at times. I can, for reasons unknown to me, find myself feeling flat, cheerless, and dreary. The joys I formerly felt yesterday, or even this morning, seem to evaporate and I'm left feeling downcast, gloomy, and alone.

It's at these times when my call to care seems a mistake. I glance at my care receiver and instead of feeling joyful, I feel dejected, no small amount of resentfulness swirls around my heart. I am losing heart; I'm feeling oppressed, slightly used, and weighted down.

I try to tell myself that these feelings are not real, they are simply inner emotional reactions to situations in my own life, or fanciful regrets of what might or could have been—hurts left unresolved, guilt or shame from the past bubbling over into today, or just random feelings that don't mean anything.

I tell myself that such feelings are not real, they are illusionary artifacts manufactured out of nothing; they are without meaning or substance or impact. More than that, I tell myself that these depressive feelings do not describe me.

I refuse to be defined by such triviality, by such whimsical nothings. I am not defined by fear, I am a child of the light, I am grounded in goodness, not evil; I breathe in the Spirit's power, I feel the warmth of the Spirit's touch, my thirst for goodness is quenched by my call to care, and I bear worthy fruits of merit and value.

SEVENTEEN

# *Because I Care... I trust in the Spirit's healing power.*

Trust surrounds me, upholds me, gives me hope, allows me to share deeply, and offers me connection to the goodness, even the sacredness of all. How I welcome trust into my life as a primary sustaining power, a sacred energy of priceless value!

Healing illness, as distinct from curing sickness, is essentially spiritual. Healing requires my care receiver to get in touch with her inner wisdom, so that her response to her illness isn't worse than her medical diagnosis.

As I go about my caregiving tasks, I sometimes feel like a farmer planting corn seed. The farmer performs so much work preparing the soil, planting the seed, watering, fertilizing, weeding, hoeing—the farmer works from dawn to dusk. But, no matter the amount of work the farmer invests in the corn, he can't make the corn grow; only trust in the Spirit's handiwork can do that.

Caregiving is much the same. I perform so many tasks. I figuratively tend the garden of my care receiver, but through it all, it is trust in the Spirit's handiwork that eventually brings healing to body, mind, and spirit. Knowing this keeps me energized, uplifted, and even inspired to go on in confidence.

I do have a mature dependence on universal love as the primary healing power. I do enjoy the Spirit's abundance and want to share it. I do experience a solid trust that good eventually "wins," and I am confident relying on the Spirit's healing hand following mine throughout my caregiving day.

Trusting fixes me firmly on solid ground, yet I take another step and can feel tremors underfoot. Ominous rumblings within me can shake my confidence and cause me to doubt the trust; this clearly disturbs the sure stability I previously felt. I can feel vulnerable and deficient; I can feel anxious and tremulous which causes me to withdraw a bit and reflexively start to protect myself—from what, I don't even know!

At such times I begin to lose my trust in trust, and I start hiding behind things like easy formulas and childish solutions to life issues. I want simple, black-and-white answers that don't involve my feelings and don't require me to think too deeply. *"Just tell me what to do, and I'll do it,"* seems to be my attitude at such times.

I reduce my call to care to a fixed set of tasks that I must perform, with or without any active emotional participation attached to them. I become an automaton, just going through the motions of caring, but not energizing or animating the tasks with any of the "real me" involved at all. Yet I trust!

EIGHTEEN

# *Because I Care…*
# *I seek the best in and for my care receiver.*

I seem to have entered a new phase in my caregiving journey. I notice the smallest things now that bring me to a new space of wonder. I rest easier when I have the sense that I am doing my best for my care receiver, when I truly know her needs and fold these into my care plan.

I pick up a towel and see the Spirit's hand at work; I see the sun streaming in the window forming a figure of light on the floor, and I think of the Spirit's magnificence; I walk down the hall and feel the presence of the Spirit; I clean the bath and detect there some aura of the fingerprint of Love; I check a monitor or fill a medications tray and right then I recognize that truth, beauty, and goodness resides there, too.

My call to care has taken on a new richness, a new patina of wonder, and a new spiritual luster that is clearly the mark of Love. I seem to see with new eyes now, certainly not all the time, but often enough to give me pause to feel a new depth of meaning emerging from the everyday tasks and common interactions I have with my care receiver.

It's as though what used to be common is no longer so. The smallest, formerly unnoticed things have now been elevated to become something very special indeed.

I marvel at this unfolding process, and, truth be known, I'm a bit embarrassed by it on the one hand, and yet, on the other, I want to broadcast it to the world that I'm living in a new realm of seeing the Spirit's presence in everything. I'm filled with a new sense of awe and don't even have the words to express it.

But I don't want to be a Pollyanna who sees everything through rose-colored glasses ... and I certainly don't! Right after I feel the presence of the Spirit, my nature, being what it is, falls back into old ways of finding fault.

I notice the defects and the imperfections; I see what should or could be, and I become critical and negative. It's hard to hold my tongue; I want so badly to point out a transgression that may be the most trivial matter of no consequence. I exert much energy trying to hold back my critique.

I'm also self-critical, and consequently I feel dejected, pessimistic, and paradoxically feel both over-qualified and under-prepared at the same time. I wonder how this can be.

But today dawns a new day, a clean slate upon which I can write a story directed by love or one directed by fear; that is my daily choice—and I want to choose the former.

NINETEEN

# *Because I Care... I regard my care receiver's feelings as important.*

So many times I wonder what's going on inside my care receiver's head, and heart, and soul; I long to know her true feelings. *"A penny for your thoughts?"* sums up quite well this curiosity of affect and thought that I feel toward my care receiver.

Healing illness involves, among many other things, opening up to who I truly am. Opening necessarily requires I see my care receiver's feelings with clear eyes.

I do wish to communicate with my care receiver at the deeper levels of closeness. I want to be totally "in touch" or "in tune" with her emotions. I wish to experience the depth of her heart and be able to "touch" her feelings. I'd like to be aware of her affective life, know where her heart is, and even emotionally "walk in her shoes."

I do have a sensitivity for the underlying motivations, the feelings that motivate the human condition and which motivate my care receiver as well. I so wish I had the time and skill necessary to engage her on this feelings level because I see feelings as so important.

Feelings are the doorway to my care receiver's heart, and this doorway leads to healing. For this reason alone, I believe it's important to engage my care receiver on a feelings level. I do feel her pain as well as delight, her desires and disappointments, and her failures and successes.

Yet I must confess that sometimes I feel a strange sensation that my heart seems to harden. I move away from feelings altogether; I find them cumbersome and sloppy, and I just want to retreat. At such times I'm sure I come across as callous and cold, unconcerned and insensitive, avoidant and distant. I don't want these feelings of course, but they impose themselves upon me quite without my permission anyway.

What's most hurtful for me is my insensitivity to myself. I can feel another's pain, but "getting in touch" with my own genuine feelings is particularly difficult for me. It seems I can be much more sensitive and caring toward my care receiver than I can be toward myself.

I know I want to be liked, and sometimes I can see what others and my care receiver wants and needs from me before they even express them; it's easy for me to act on my "emotional hunches," to provide for the emotional needs almost above all else.

I do have emotional insight with almost everyone but myself. I understand the motivations of others but I'm somewhat blind to my own.

I long for a deep self-knowledge and know that the path there is obviously through the strength of empathy, another of the Spirit's sacred healing virtues.

## TWENTY

# *Because I Care… I am grateful to be of service.*

It has been said that the greatest prayer is a simple yet profound, "Thank you." Here is the spiritual place where I want to reside in my caregiving.

I am grateful for the opportunity to express my unique gifts—gifts that may not have surfaced to this degree had I not answered the call to care. I'm grateful also for the celestial motivating force of grace that gives life to my gifts of care; I could not carry on without this energy.

At times I feel I'm participating in a holy play where I'm both an actor and an observer. I act in unmerited divine assistance from my Higher Power, and I observe in reverent praise for what is. I feel edified and spiritually filled, even sanctified by all this abundance. My feelings grow much bigger and grander than simple appreciation; they expand at times to amazement and awe.

Caregiving helps me refocus what's most important in life; it gives me a new data set, a new perspective that allows me to think clearer. It invigorates a new sense of gratitude in me.

But I guard against letting my deep gratitude evaporate, as it sometimes can do, leaving a void in me where I find the opposite of gratitude in its place, a place of blame that emerges in me from time to time. For some curious reason I can sometimes adopt an edge of blame in my voice.

For reasons unknown to me I can become sharp and even pointed in my interactions with my care receiver; I get critical and can even lay guilt upon her. I overlook gratitude and goodness; I can even reject it.

I can ridicule my care receiver, which at first only scares her, and then leads to an emotional standoff where she might return my ridicule by lashing out at me in some way, after adopting an uncooperative attitude toward me. Initially I get mad at this but quickly realize the part I have played in generating this retaliatory behavior.

Yet, it's the other side of gratitude that bites me more. I devalue my gratitude to a distorted level when I become submissive, feeling unworthy to be in the place and condition that I am. I'm over-grateful to the point where I overwork and over-do. I can become almost fawning and servile in my attempts to prove my worth or make up for some illusionary inadequacies about me.

I adopt a personal inferior posture that makes me feel overly indebted to others and certainly out-of-sync with my true self. I know this is not "who" or "what" I truly am, yet I confess that such feelings do visit me from time to time, however fleetingly. Again I try to fly back to genuine gratitude at my personality center... at my core, and find peace.

TWENTY-ONE

# *Because I Care… I seek to be a harmonizing influence.*

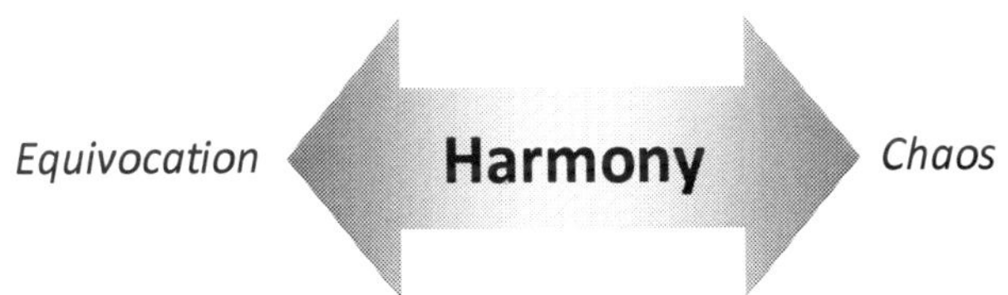

I need harmony in my life. I prefer peace to contention, order over disorder, and working together rather than division. When harmony exists, I simply feel better.

I strive to bring this harmony into my caregiving as well. I want my caregiving to flow, to move along smoothly; I don't like surprises that throw off my established routines of efficiency, and I don't like change for change sake.

I like operating in accordance with central principles that provide organization, integration, and even wholeness in my life and my caregiving. I like to be 'in sync' with my under-girding principles of peace; I like to build a plan and work that plan to completion.

Most of all, I need to know that my caregiving work is aligned with my values of peace, and that it fits together with an overall order from my Higher Power. Caregiving requires harmony generating practices, all of which center around internal order, cohesion, and integration. I take note of my care receiver's "self-talk" because positive self-talk enhances illness healing, negative self-talk does the opposite.

Naturally my preference for harmony is only seldom achieved. I fall in disorder regularly. Harmony leaves me when my care receiver isn't particularly cooperative or simply out-of-sorts to the point of being contrary. There are times when my care receiver and I might not agree; indeed, we differ on many points. This disagreement, too, can cause me to lose my internal compass.

I can get befuddled and confused; my mind seems to lack clarity at times, and all my plans seem quite insufficient. It's at these times when I lapse into a tangle of indecision—I hesitate for lack of direction. I seem to lose my normal clear-headed focus and find myself walking through a swamp of over-thinking everything.

My indecision about doing what's 'right' causes me such confusion that I don't do anything. I procrastinate; I do the easy "no brainer" tasks and put off anything that requires a decision.

I seem to be trapped in a morass of hesitancy and frustration, a conundrum of equivocation. I simply can't discern the best course because I fear making a mistake.

One of my big problems, of course, liking harmony as I do, is trying to please everyone. I can go round and round in a decision-making quandary trying to figure out the perfect solution for all concerned. I've noticed that it's generally me who winds up in disharmony. I please everyone but myself.

Harmony is illusive, and perfect harmony is impossible. But I take solace knowing that while I can't achieve perfect harmony in my caregiving, perfect harmony does exist in the Spirit whom I talk with regularly.

## TWENTY-TWO

# *Because I Care…*
# *I can be patient and also responsive.*

Why is patience so hard for me? Why is waiting for my care receiver to finish her meal or even finish a sentence so exasperating for me? I do work on my patience.

I've counted to 10 a hundred times; I've talked to myself, blamed myself, denigrated myself, and even distracted myself attempting to build patience. But none of these work very well for me. I still want to demand action now.

I admit that I confuse patience with waiting, and waiting with inefficiency and consequently ineffectiveness. Wasting time is somehow 'sinful,' it violates something deeply tucked away inside me. Yet caregiving excellence is quite impossible without big helpings of patience. I know I need to learn to find the sacred calm that exists in me.

I want to smoothly surmount interruptions and continue on peacefully even in the face of disorder. I want to bound over any inner impulses to lose my temper, or at least my inner calm. I want to transform annoyance into another opportunity to be strongly calm. I want to discover and remain in that still point of tranquility all day long, that sacred place in me where the Spirit resides. I want to keep a calm smile on my face and a cool (but not cold) demeanor about me. I want to flow downstream through my caregiving day and not have to fight my way upstream.

The soft inner voice of healing speaks to me in its own language. I can achieve all this at times, but it's hard. My best tactic to remain patient is to make an intentional decision early in the day that today will be a day of peace, that I can handle whatever comes along today, that the Spirit is always there ready to give me yet another shot of patience upon request, and that I will be at peace.

Enlightened caregiving is patient so I can listen deeply to the message of hope. What is the central message of my care receiver's illness and of my caregiving? I'm trying to train myself to be more patient by keeping the prayer-like mantra, *"I am patient and calm,"* continuously "running" in the background of my mind—this does help a lot.

But I need to guard against slipping into a sluggish mode; I don't want my budding patience to slow me down—that's not patience, it's a form of unresponsiveness. Patience actually allows me to work smarter rather than harder; it gives me an inner peace that bolsters my confidence and enhances my work effectiveness. Most of all, patience allows me to glide through my day calmly so that I'm actually more, and not less, on top of my caregiving 'game.'

## TWENTY-THREE

# *Because I Care…*
# *I can be strong for my care receiver.*

I think I pray for strength more than anything else. I cry out to the Spirit, "*Lord, give me strength!*" Yet this is not a hollow lament, it's a genuine request to receive the grace-power that already exists in me, but which seems to dissolve much too easily.

I need to be strong for my care receiver, but to do so I need to discover my own internal strength. Caregiving requires strength. I do need to be a decision maker and a change agent to fully honor my call to caregiving—these take strength.

I need the stamina to walk the next caregiving mile, to plod on even in the face of difficulties. Caregiving causes me to expend my physical, emotional, and spiritual energies. What I want most, even though I may not be aware of it, is strength.

I need to be vigorous and develop the capacity for sustained exertion—I need to be strong. I need the competency of being able to gather myself back up after I've been knocked down, to reassemble myself after I've been broken down.

I need to resist the temptation to be the victim by regaining my natural and innate capacity for action. Illness gives my care receiver the opportunity to re-meet the Spirit within—not as a set of dogma or as in weary recitations of prayers lines memorized from youth, but re-meet the Spirit as alive and fresh and vital for facing the life challenge that now confronts her.

I need to tell myself over and over that I will get back up when I fall, I will eventually succeed even though I may sometimes fail. I can develop new resolve, new vigor, and new direction. But I can't do this by myself... I need the Spirit's help.

To do this, I need to be ever mindful that my power comes from above. I know how weak I can be, especially when I lose sight of my center point that is strength-abundant. I let little things overpower my usual determination; I can forfeit my naturally strong nature, the one implanted in me by the Spirit, to the many distractions of the day.

I overly focus on those things I can't do well, and take for granted what I can do well. I get exhausted and lose my momentum; this dispirits me much too easily. I pray for resolve, and direction, and determination, and energy.

Yet I can't go overboard or even pervert my strength into some heavy-handed and forced way of acting. I can exercise my strength and power without resorting to force. I show my strength more by my inner power than by grand outward displays of manipulation or control.

I am strong and I need to use my strength in caregiving but I also need to be delicate, and sensible, and articulate in all that I do. Caring means that I can be strong but also tender; I'm called to be tough at times, but also compassionate.

The more experience I gather caregiving the more I realize just how demanding and yet, oh so rewarding this curious calling of caregiving can be for me.

## TWENTY-FOUR

# *Because I Care... I am "fully with" my care receiver and with the Spirit at the same time.*

*Unreality* **Transcendence** *Worldliness*

As I mature in my caregiving and in trust of myself, I realize ever more clearly that my caregiving excellence demands that I become aware of all the dimensions of living simultaneously.

Certainly I'm called to be vigilant to all of my care receiver's physical needs. Here rests the fundamentals of caregiving, the absolute essentials. Yet the physical care needs need no particular discernment because they are generally so apparent. These include adequate food, clothing, shelter, medical care, proper rest, etc. These are the mandatory requirements of my care receiver.

But she has many more needs, different levels of needs of which I need to be aware. My care receiver has psycho-emotional needs including: socialization, feeling useful, having worth, time management, knowledge of the aging process, being heard and understood, having a close friend, etc. While I'm not responsible for fulfilling all these needs, I do need to be aware of them.

Finally, my care receiver has spiritual needs. I want to be very cognizant of these, all of which surround the notion of extracting meaning from life right now, meaning that goes beyond the material and occupational levels.

Caregiving tests my personality to its limits, it confronts me with my shadows and compulsions like nothing else, but it also points the way to immense spiritual growth like nothing else can.

I live in two worlds with my care receiver—the light and the dark sides at the same time. Addressing all her needs means that I must first be aware of the range of human needs, and second, I need to bring them into conversation however minimally. I must "live" on all three levels: physical, mental, and especially the spiritual with its accent on "being" rather than on "doing."

Caregiving requires my *being with* my care receiver just as much as *doing for* her. I'm aware of the spiritual dimensions of life and consequently do what I can to include references, questions, observations, etc., that have to do with life meaning.

I try to reframe any of my care receiver's statements that refer to lifelessness, despondency, futility, alienation, worthlessness, and the like. Such emotions go beyond the psychological level and edge into the spiritual since they involve the ultimate meaning of living.

I can't confine myself to only one arena; I must include all three, 1) physical, 2) psycho-emotional, and 3) spiritual in order to pursue caregiving excellence. I need to be grounded in the material reality, be aware of emotional needs, and find inspiration in the spiritual arena.

TWENTY-FIVE

# *Because I Care… I discipline myself.*

*Self-Repression* **Self-Discipline** *Self-Indulgence*

Caregiving certainly requires order. Tasks are best accomplished on a time schedule. They need to be regularized, efficiently executed, and accomplished thoroughly with necessary follow-through. I want to be organized enough to initiate and maintain all of these requirements.

When order is absent, then chaos ensues. All this takes a keen and advanced self-discipline on my part. I cannot adequately answer my call to caregiving without the requisite self-control, maintenance of focus, and attention to detail.

The basic question of illness healing is, "*Do I want to be well?*" I need to bolster this spirit of resolve in my care receiver as best I can; I also need to do this for myself—this takes tremendous discipline.

Self-discipline means that I learn well how to enforce obedience from one part of me onto another. One side of me tends to be lazy, but another side wants to be successful. Self-discipline is the force that allows the successful side to override the lazy side thereby replacing tendencies of laziness with ones of productivity.

Caregiving calls every part of my personality to come together to achieve a goal. The call to care is not effortless; on the contrary it requires that all parts of my personality act together with smooth, effective agility.

Naturally self-discipline imposes the internal order required to achieve the desired results. Self-discipline is creative; it organizes resources, both personal and material, in new ways to achieve desired care goals. Self-discipline motivates me, and keeps me on-track all day long.

Without self-discipline, I can lapse into a semi-idleness or sluggishness that robs me of feeling good about myself and about my caregiving work. Self-discipline can unravel into self-indulgence quickly when my willpower, personal order, and internal obedience slowly evaporate to a point where both my care receiver and my own motivation suffer.

I can daydream, make little excuses, blame someone else for not preparing or supporting me, claim I lack the resources to do an adequate job, compare myself to others who I think aren't doing their share, etc. All these are self-deceptive excuses that invade my self-discipline and vastly decelerate my forward movement.

When I catch myself fading, I sometimes over-react by pushing too hard or by imposing overly strict expectations upon myself. These seldom last long, and I find I easily lapse into a lack of self-control once again.

I've discovered that I'm a poor regulator of my self-discipline; I found that my best reason for discipline doesn't come from me, but that its best source is the Spirit in me. I must invoke this special grace-power to keep me, and my care receiver moving optimally.

TWENTY-SIX

# *Because I Care…*
# *I try to seek and speak the truth.*

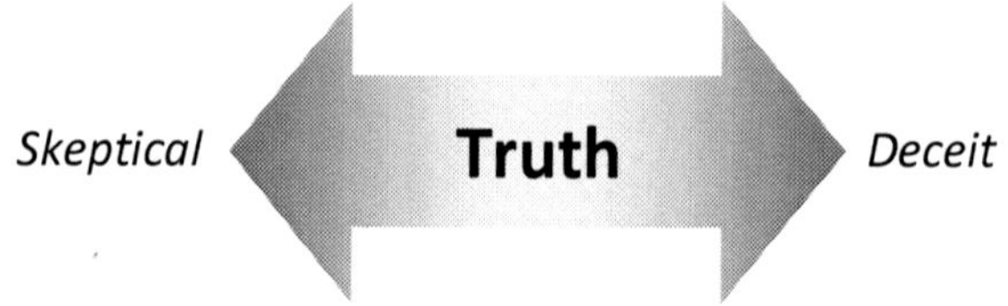

Of course I want to be truthful, I don't want to deceive anyone, and I don't want to deceive myself. I owe it to my care receiver to be completely up front with her.

Yet, being truthful is much more than not lying. Truth means that I base my life on the solid rock of core principles that provide both the foundation and the light for action.

Caregiving invites me into an adventure both brutal and miraculous. Yet what voice do I listen to, which one do I favor—the truth of the dying, that of fear, or the truth of the thriving, that of love?

Living with integrity means I remain true to these underlying principles, and my behavior reflects what I believe to be true. When I am true to myself I am fair, genuine, and authentically "me."

Truth calls me to be real in the sense that what I project I am by my behavior is who I truly am; I'm free of internal and external deception. Truth calls me to be honest with myself and honest with others as well as my care receiver. When I'm honest I can share myself openly and form care bonds characterized by genuineness and sincerity.

It's hard being truthful of speech and truthful of self. My care receiver knows at some level (even when I don't) when I'm not truthful; she knows if I'm even slightly misleading or circumventing or manipulating the absolute truth. There are very few times when I intentionally try to shade the truth about my caregiving tasks, yet I may not be aware of how I might shade my own truth by thinking or projecting something I'm not.

I may do this, quite without my awareness, when I doubt my abilities, when I over-question myself, and especially if my self-skepticism creates even the smallest thought that I'm not what I appear to be. When I allow thoughts like these to grab hold, I undermine my confidence, damage my composure, and inject unnecessary clutter into my mind.

I hide the truth about who and what I am—that I am full and complete and whole, and that at my core I reflect truth, beauty, and goodness of my spiritual strengths. These strengths, the best of the universe has to offer, pulsate through me.

Certainly I have lots to learn, and my innate talents, gifts, and strengths need constant updating and support. But the terrible self-skepticism that I sometimes allow to take capture me diverts my energies away from the caregiving issues at hand and tosses me into a swirl of self-uncertainty.

I'm not living my truth when I let this happen; I'm spun out into a deceitful space of insecurity. Once again I'm called to my true center, that place of peace and trust and honesty in me that is truly me. It is this truth that sets me free.

## TWENTY-SEVEN

# *Because I Care… I seek to bring an inpiring heart to every care receiver encounter.*

Am I an inspired caregiver? What am I inspiring—what am I breathing in? Because what I breathe in is what I will expire—breathe out.

I want the best for my care receiver and for me, but to give the best I must take in, inspire, the best. Again, what am I breathing into my soul? Is it the best or not?

To be inspired means that I'm infused with light and life, I'm motivated by the best most noble and life-filled forces available. I'm touched by a special power that energizes me and brings life to my actions.

In my caregiving, I feel inspired when I realize that I'm part of the celestial mechanisms of healing care that come from above, that I am supported by the Spirit's grace and power so that I can extend my hand as a healing force to my care receiver.

Yes, to bring inspiration to my care receiver, to give it, I must inspire, breathe in what is inspiring, what in-spirits me. I'm not a miracle worker, but with inspiration I can offer the wonder of inspiration to my care receiver.

The degree to which I don't or can't breathe in goodness and strength is the same degree to which I find myself uninspired. I can sometimes feel somewhat deadened, without vigor, lacking in spirit, feeling all my senses dampened, and my life without luster.

Without inspiration I just go through the caregiving motions; I bring no special anything into the caregiving room. I'm simply "there." Without inspiration I feel somewhat numb and passive, dull and dreary, and my actions are expressionless.

When I don't or can't seem to tap into some form of inspiration, my caregiving is flat and my life seems "on hold."

Sometimes I try to compensate for my inspiration poverty by forcing myself to move at hyper-warp speed. I crave to be super-busy, hyper-stimulated, and perpetually aroused. I can do this for a time, but eventually I get agitated, nervous, anxious, and I can't relax. I can't let go—I'm going a thousand miles per hour. I'm hyperventilating, gulping very thin air trying to find some true inspiration somewhere.

This is clearly not the answer I want; it's uncomfortable for me, and upsetting for my care receiver.

Caregiving can make my heart come to life; it allows me to rediscover myself, a true revitalization of spirit. It's my job to somehow pass this new inspiration along to my care receiver. Where is my true inspiration, how can I breathe deeply and fill my soul with truly refreshing and inspiring air?

Caregiving is my classroom for learning the answer. I need to remind myself to consciously and intentionally breathe in the best from my caregiving. I need to focus in and breathe the truth, beauty, and goodness that are there. When I can do this, I'm confident that I will be genuinely inspired.

## TWENTY-EIGHT

# *Because I Care...*
# *I strive to be kind and compassionate always.*

My best caregiving actions are motivated by kindness and compassion. I want my care behaviors to not only reflect kindness but to be kind and compassionate.

I know that my care receiver does better when I inject gentleness, attentiveness, and mercy into my care behaviors. The better I can genuinely demonstrate these qualities along with tenderness, friendliness, and helpfulness, the better she responds to my care, the better I feel about what I do, and equally important, the better I feel about myself.

I am a caregiving. I give care, and my best care is shot through with courtesy, goodwill, understanding, and empathy. Compassion is a most fortifying tool for healing. I want to employ compassion not simply as a logical device or technical tool, but as a natural expression of the heart—the magnet pull of divine love and true beauty. I do know all this, yet making this a reality of my everyday care is more than challenging.

I fall into the doldrums of indifference at times—even when I try hard to avoid it. I get tired and weary, and I can sometimes lose interest. I find myself violating basic kindness; I can cut corners and even, at times, disregard basic caregiving requirements. I can ignore my care receiver. Others around me may not notice my indifference, but I do. I do only the bare minimum to get by.

I look busy perhaps, but I'm just getting through the day with little or no kindness and compassion folded into my caregiving mix. My heart is not *in* my work, or maybe I just lose heart a bit. But there are other times when I feel quite differently.

I seem to take my motivation and my energy not from the deep spirit well within me, but from my care receiver herself. I seem to need my care receiver to need me. I seem to need her presence as much as she needs mine. Consequently I'm a bit excessive in the amount of care I offer and the manner in which I offer it.

My need seems inappropriate; I've crossed some boundary of professional integrity, at least on an emotional level, by becoming oddly dependent on my care receiver. Such behavior is over-the-top beyond kindness; it's a distortion of compassion.

Some amount of this I believe is acceptable, but I'm still unsure exactly where the line between giving genuine, kind, and compassionate care stops, and where dependent care begins.

I know that I need to persist in my daily attempts to practice real kindness and genuine compassion consistently. I need to spend a moment or two each day in a quiet posture of reverence asking for the grace of kindness to be with me all day. This practice is kindness care for me.

TWENTY-NINE

# *Because I Care…*
# *I strive to show courage under stressful conditions.*

Caregiving is a courageous endeavor. It takes a unique mental and moral internal fortitude to face the perils of the call to care. I need to find the courage to meet the demands and uncertainties of caring.

Caregiving requires that I regularly put myself "on the line," or even "in harm's way." For all this I require the mental and spiritual bracing of courage. I need to be resilient so I can hold up under fire. I need courage to avoid the temptation to give care without caring.

Caregiving can be difficult, my character is tested daily, my will is challenged, and my tenacity questioned. I need courage to stand tall in front of all of this. Courageous caregiving calls me to rise above all my self-focused desires and shift my gaze to the farther horizon of what's best for my care receiver.

Confidence comes from courage mixed with dashes of faith and trust. Confidence is not simply bequeathed to me by knowing the tasks of my job. Courage provides me with personality hardiness, which steels me so I can stand up to adversity and the many disappointments that can punctuate my day.

When I have courage, I am dauntless. But I don't always have courage, and even when I do, it seems I possess it in only meager amounts. I don't always boldly march forth in parade-like determination. I can be the opposite of bold; I can shrink in fear of the unknown lurking just around the corner.

I admit to fear at times; I can be easily frightened: looking stupid, being a failure, overlooking necessary tasks, incurring the wrath or disapproval of others/supervisors, being ignored by family/staff, losing my edge, etc., etc.

Sometimes I just emotionally stick my head in the sand. And what I do to try to hide such timidity scares me even more—I take on a false superior and even condescending attitude of, "*I know what*

*I'm doing*." As I look at this I see it simply as a defensive cover-up of my fear. It seems an extension of the old adage that, "*The best defense is a good offense.*"

But I fear the behaviors that flow from this attitude may be offensive and even hurtful to my care receiver and those around me. I can become a bit over-bearing and a bit "full of myself"—both of which I don't like but they still remain strangely compelling.

This mask I wear creates a false presentation of me; it's not my real me, only some inaccurate facsimile of me. It doesn't feel real, and I know this even as I'm acting it out, but I feel almost powerless to modify it.

I know that nothing is impossible with the Spirit, and so it's the Spirit whom I consult for guidance, counsel, and the power to change.

THIRTY

---

# *Because I Care…*
# *I stay the course… I don't easily give up.*

---

*Imperilousness* **Perseverance** *Giving up*

Caregiving seems endless—an uninterrupted assembly line of tasks to perform, people to consult, data to gather and track and report, money to manage, charts to assemble, notations to make, phone calls and e-mails and instant messages, and even tweets to attend to, etc., etc. On and on the conveyor belt rolls along with apparently no let up.

To keep up, and to keep going, I need the strength of perseverance, the ability to keep on keeping on. I need to be persistent in my resolve, and keep putting one foot in front of the other—plodding on and plodding on always reaching to achieve the goal, fulfill the mission, and satisfy the caregiving vision.

But my caregiving job is never finished—it's never all done, which makes it even more difficult to stay the course with caring excellence. Staying the course also means that I help my care receiver remain vitally alive and not "die" of her emotional reaction to illness, even though she survives physically. I want to let down my stamina just a bit; I want to give my meager and tired tenacity a small vacation; I want to let my intense focus drift ever so slightly—I want to take a break from the vigilance of purpose

Yet, I'm called to achieve. I can get so tired at times that I hear a little interior voice encouraging me to just give up. Surprisingly this gives me a little solace; just the prospect of letting go of the responsibility is most appealing. But, of course, I do need to "stay the course."

I want to surrender, to terminate; there are even those infrequent times when I'd love to "throw in the towel." It's not that I want to go away forever, or abandon my post, but I would find a short vacation just so wonderfully refreshing. So I tell myself to simply buckle down and not buckle under the stress and strain of it all.

But then I get a strange notion that I may be using my perseverance unwisely. Is it possible to cross a bridge from active perseverance to an inactive place of putting myself in danger, to "go down with the ship" even if I don't have to?

If I do carry forth and do, and do, and do some more, might I not eventually push myself so far, that I do place myself in unnecessary peril and risk damaging not only my call to caregiving but also my very self in the process?

I can throw caution to the wind and unknowingly march on into the personal peril of overwork. I can disregard my own well-being in body, mind, and spirit and wind up the less for it.

True perseverance comes only from the superpower of love, and love will always see me through—sometimes by telling me to stop!

# Postscript

Caregiving, in whatever setting, is a call to become more of who you actually are. This call is sometimes faint, sometimes almost lost in the clangs and bangs of the caregiving day. Though you are pressed, you strive to find the silent moment when you can collect yourself and reflect on the meaning of what you're about; it's not simply about getting through the day (although some days that seems to be all you're longing for), more than this, caregiving is about finding you, becoming the full you, discovering your wholeness.

Wholeness refers to a state of personal integration. When you are whole, when you're at your best, you have personal integrity. Your personality achieves integration when all the pieces of your life structure are cohesively held together by unifying principles. This integration or wholeness allows you to live with an overriding sense of peace that this world cannot give. There is a transcendent or transpersonal (out of this world) quality to caregivers who are approaching wholeness. They live in this world, but they find their wholeness by investing spiritual energy (their spiritual strengths) that comes from out of this world.

There are four characteristics of caregivers who are approaching wholeness:

1. Balance. Caregivers pursuing wholeness give their personal life energy to all the arenas of their life, not just to one or two. They see their "life job" as building the very best person from the raw materials they have been given by God and through genetic selection. They are well rounded, not personality lop-sided. They grow fully, like a tree that

gets abundant amounts of water and light; it's not spindly or crooked; rather, it's straight, strong, and well structured.

2. Direction. Whole caregivers derive generous amounts of life meaning from their lives because they have a life purpose, a goal that is bigger than they are. They live their life "on purpose," recognizing that the meaning that flows from their life purpose can be the greatest generator of health, wellness, and happiness they can have. They are generally people of faith, and recognize that their belief system is at the center of their purpose.

3. Being Positive. Wholeness includes developing the means and skills necessary to keep their overall morale high. They recognize that they themselves, and not anyone else or any outside forces, are responsible for their own happiness. They seem to keep themselves happy. They develop a certain detachment from the ills of their bodies, and of the world. They don't focus exclusively on worldly matters, but raise their view to things beyond this world as well.

4. Show Their Light. Caregivers with wholeness view their life experiences as life advantages rather than as weights pulling them down. They know they have gifts and talents, and without being in the least bit boastful, they let their inner light shine. They generate a kind of spiritual luster by appreciating their internal attractiveness, and making friends with their uniqueness.

I invite all caregivers to take the Spiritual Strengths Healing Profile (SSHP) and to participate in the Spiritual Strengths Caregiving Program. You can find out more at:

*www.SpiritualStrengthsHealing.com*